PAST   PRESENT

NOE VALLEY

Opposite: The iconic image from the neighborhood's past is the classic sign at the corner of Noe and Valley Streets. The sign seen here has since been replaced by one that includes lowercase lettering, and the building in the background has been altered. (WPY.)

Past　Present

NOE VALLEY

Bill Yenne

Copyright © 2019 by Bill Yenne
ISBN 978-1-4671-0375-6

Library of Congress Control Number: 2019935723

Published by Arcadia Publishing
Charleston, South Carolina

Printed in the United States of America

For all general information, please contact Arcadia Publishing:
Telephone 843-853-2070
Fax 843-853-0044
E-mail sales@arcadiapublishing.com
For customer service and orders:
Toll-Free 1-888-313-2665

Visit us on the Internet at www.arcadiapublishing.com

Visit the author at www.BillYenne.com

On the Front Cover: The intersection of Twenty-Fourth and Castro Streets has always been one of the key transit hubs in Noe Valley. In 1938, it was a Market Street Railway cable car line that crossed the hill to and from Market Street, and today it is the San Francisco Municipal Railway's No. 24 Divisadero bus line. (Noe Valley Archives/Bill Yenne.)

On the Back Cover: This young lady attracted quite the crowd when she tackled the Duncan Street Hill in her touring car around 1923. The street was long ago superseded by pedestrian steps. (Noe Valley Archives.)

Contents

Acknowledgments		vii
Introduction		viii
1.	The Twenty-Fourth Street Corridor	11
2.	North of Twenty-Fourth	35
3.	The Church Street Corridor	47
4.	Southward into Upper Noe	57
5.	Selected Noe Valley Maps	93

Acknowledgments

The author is grateful to the many people throughout Noe Valley who have been supportive of his more than four decades of recording and chronicling the historic legacy of this unique neighborhood, and of the city, in such books as his 1998 best-seller, *San Francisco Then & Now*, and his popular 2004 book, *San Francisco's Noe Valley*. For the historical images in this book, a special tip of the hat must be extended to the late Paul Kantus (1926–2008), a lifetime neighborhood resident, whose Noe Valley Archives (NVA) collection was utilized by this author for both *San Francisco's Noe Valley* and the present work. In turn, thanks are due Joel Panzer for taking it upon himself to preserve Paul's collection after Paul passed away.

The author also wishes to thank and acknowledge his family, including his daughters, who grew up in Noe Valley, and his three grandsons, who are growing up here now.

Special thanks are due Woody LaBounty, who generously provided access to historical images from the collection of the Western Neighborhoods Project (WNP), which includes, among other treasures, pictures that originated with the Department of Public Works (DPW). The contemporary images are, unless noted, by and copyright Bill Yenne (WPY). The four sets of initials in parentheses on this page are used in the majority of the picture credits within the book.

Introduction

Noe Valley, often called the "Village within the City," is a charming and friendly residential neighborhood in the heart of San Francisco. Indeed, the geographic center of the city and county of San Francisco is within Noe Valley. It is known for its warm and friendly ambience, its coffee shops, good schools, weekly farmer's market, pleasant walking streets crowded with independent retail shops, and nice people.

Geographically, Noe Valley is generally accepted to be bounded on the west by Grand View Avenue or Douglass Street, on the north by Twenty-Second Street, on the east by Dolores Street, and on the south by Thirtieth Street. The boundaries are informal and there are variations. For example, they are occasionally pushed eastward to Guerrero Street and south to Laidley Street, etc. The main business corridor is Twenty-Fourth Street, roughly between Diamond Street and Church Street, but by some reckoning it may be stretched a block or two either way. Twenty-Fourth has Noe Valley's only two traffic lights. Church Street, from Twenty-Second Street to Thirtieth, is also an important commercial corridor, offering a mix of shops and eateries south of Twenty-Fourth Street. On Church Street, which has Noe Valley's only light rail line, one will encounter the regularly scheduled J Church streetcar, as well as cars from the San Francisco Municipal Railway's historic streetcar fleet making their way north from the Geneva Yards to their own scheduled runs along Market Street and the Embarcadero.

This book highlights these corridors and is divided between the areas north and south of Twenty-Fourth, much of the latter being known as "Upper Noe." Like the neighborhood as a whole, the boundaries of Upper Noe are open to interpretation. Today, Twenty-Sixth or Twenty-Seventh Streets are usually named as Upper Noe's northern boundary, but in 1959, the Upper Noe History Committee put it at Twenty-Fifth. They also extended Upper Noe's southeast corner to Miguel Street and San Jose Avenue, which would have absorbed territory now considered part of the Glen Park and Mission districts.

Noe Valley evolved from a portion of the old Rancho San Miguel land grant owned by José de Jesús Noé (1805–1862), who was twice the alcalde (mayor) of Yerba Buena, the settlement that became the city of San Francisco in 1847. The Noe Valley street grid was laid out in the Victorian era of the 19th century by John Meirs Horner (1821–1907), who arrived in California in 1846 with the group of Mormons led by Sam Brannan, the newspaperman who became famous for publishing the news that sparked the Gold Rush of 1849.

Horner acquired part of Rancho San Miguel from Noé in 1854, subdivided the land into blocks and lots, named it Horner's Addition, and gave names to the streets, some reflecting his family ties and his Mormon faith. Many of these names remain today, but some were changed to numbers by 1870 (see the map on page 93). For instance, in Horner's vision, Twenty-Fourth Street was originally "Park Street," while Twenty-Second, Alvarado, and Twenty-Third were originally "John," "M," and "Horner!" Elizabeth Street, named for Horner's wife, remains. Being a Mormon, he named present Twenty-Fifth as "Temple," and Church, Sanchez, Noe, and Castro were once "Silver," "Cristal [sp]," "Pearl," and "Diamond." When Horner's Diamond became Castro Street, the present Diamond Street was added one block west.

Horner lost his fortune in the economic collapse of 1857, liquidated his holdings, and eventually headed to Hawaii. However, his neighborhood was built. The vast profusion of Victorian-era homes in Noe Valley, which survived the great earthquakes of 1906 and 1989, are his legacy and help define the character of Noe Valley architecture.

Another Victorian-era historical event came when the Pioneer, the first automobile to be produced on the West Coast, was built here in 1896. J.A. Meyer, a German machinist and engineer, created the vehicle in a garage at 4181 Twenty-Fourth Street that is still owned by the Meyer family. The Pioneer itself is now part of the Oakland Museum collection.

Noe Valley was the longtime home of sculptor Ruth Asawa (1926–2013), one of San Francisco's greatest artists. She was also a proponent of art education as an empowering experience, especially for children. In 1968, she started an arts program at Alvarado School in Noe Valley that evolved into the citywide San Francisco Arts Education Project. The huge 30-foot mural in the Alvarado schoolyard is a fitting reminder of her pioneering work with the Alvarado Arts Program and the other such programs throughout the city.

For its first 100 years or so, Noe Valley was a typical multiethnic working class family neighborhood, and by the middle 20th century it was also being discovered by artists and writers. The turn of the present century saw a growing number of families involved in the tech industry in San Francisco and Silicon Valley.

In the evolution of the neighborhood through the last century, there have been the inevitable changes. Noe Valley was once home to five gas stations, four on Twenty-Fourth Street alone. None survive. Some changes are lamentable. Sawyer's Hardware, which opened in 1898 and became Tuggey's Hardware a year later, survived for 114 years before closing. Once there were several movie theaters, including the grand Noe, a classic movie palace on Twenty-Fourth Street that entertained patrons from 1937 to 1952. Four supermarkets dwindled to one, Bell Market, which is now Whole Foods.

On the other hand, as businesses go, businesses also come. In the middle of the 20th century, kids were spending their allowances at Glen Five & Ten and Meyer's Variety. When my own kids were growing up, the places to go were East of the Sun and the amazing Star Magic, while their children enjoyed going to The Ark. Many businesses have stood the test of time. The gift store, Just for Fun, and Small Frys children's store have been around since the 1980s.

And so it is with restaurants and watering holes. The classic diner known as Herb's Fine Foods existed in the 3900 block of Twenty-Fourth Street from 1943 to 2007 and became so popular with people involved in neighborhood affairs, that for a time it seemed like it was Noe Valley's defacto city hall. Today, the site is home to the well-liked Toast Eatery. The location of Speckmann's German deli and restaurant on Church Street would later be occupied by Uma Casa, a Portuguese restaurant. We cannot forget the unforgettable Bud's Ice Cream. Bud Scheideman opened the business in 1933, and his cousin Bud Edlin took over in 1952. The latter Bud passed away in 2008. We remember lines of customers up the block. At this same location, on the corner of Castro and Twenty-Fourth, Subs Inc. now carries on the tradition by serving Mitchell's Ice Cream, made on nearby San Jose Avenue since 1953.

Today, the upscale Firefly Restaurant has earned great reviews and stood the test of time since 1994. When it comes to coffee shops, family-owned Martha and Brothers dates back to 1987 and has locations on both Twenty-Fourth and Church. A time traveler from the 1970s or before would certainly recognize the Haystack Pizza Restaurant and The Peaks bar. Some familiar spots survive after having had a succession of names. The Valley Tavern on Twenty-Fourth would be familiar to a visitor from the past who remembers it as Finnegan's Wake, or as the Rat and Raven. With bookstores, we recall Cover-to-Cover, while now enjoying Folio Books, where the frequency of interesting and entertaining events for all ages has made it a centerpiece of neighborhood energy.

Neighborhood life is also enriched by such institutions as our monthly neighborhood newspaper, the *Noe Valley Voice*, which was begun in 1977 by Jack Tipple and Sally Smith, and by the Noe Valley Ministry, where the Noe Valley Chamber Music Association brings world-class musicians to the neighborhood. Important annual events include the two-day St. Philip's Parish Festival, held every September for over 75 years, the neighborhood Garden Tour, and Book Week, run by literary enthusiast Richard May. Seasonal events include the annual Easter egg hunts and free hayrides, which are favorites of the kids. Halloween in Noe Valley finds a parade of children on Twenty-Fourth Street, as families enjoy the typically warm evening and the treats offered by businesses and residents throughout the neighborhood.

In 2003, the Noe Valley Farmer's Market was started in a parking lot on Twenty-Fourth Street near Vicksburg. Leslie Crawford, Paula Benton, Peter Gabel and other hardworking volunteers created what has become a regular community event now run by Elizabeth Crane. Each Saturday, people crowd through booths selecting fresh produce, enjoying musicians, and catching up with their neighbors. Another group of neighbors, including Todd David, Chris Keene, and Leslie Crawford raised funds to transform this parking lot into the Noe Valley Town Square, which hosts regular events for the community to enjoy.

In 2005, neighborhood groups, including the Noe Valley Merchants and Professionals Association and Friends of Noe Valley, spearheaded by Friends president Debra Neiman, and local business owners Carol Yenne, Bob Roddick, David Eiland, and Robert Ramsey came together to create a special use district to maintain the cleanliness, beauty, and function of the Noe Valley shopping district. As a result, the Twenty-Fourth Street commercial corridor is now one of the most admired in the city.

When people learn that I've been around Noe Valley for more than four decades, I am often asked about the changes. However, my first thought, and this can be seen in these pages, is how little it has changed. For example, back in the 1940s, Johnny McCarthy was hosting programs for kids at his gas station, which stood on exactly the same spot as the Noe Valley Town Square. Up the street, the space at Twenty-Fourth and Noe occupied by the Greek restaurant Panos for the last two decades of the last century would later be occupied by Novy, started by the daughters of the original Panos owners. The list goes on. The names may have changed, in some cases several times, but Noe Valley's commercial corridors are still vibrant, with a high value placed on independent locally owned businesses.

On the residential streets that climb through the surrounding hills and dales, one has only to look at the distinctive architecture and realize that many of the homes can be seen in both the past and present pictures in this book. In many parts of Noe Valley, the only visual changes in half a century, or even a century, are the paint color on the buildings and the presence of a lot more trees. Though there is a struggle with the San Francisco Planning Department, which encourages modern architecture, rather than the Victorian style that has defined Noe Valley, the classic Victorians remain in the majority, and the character of the neighborhood remains intact.

Change? Well, there has been quite a bit, but Noe Valley is still Noe Valley, where the more things change, the more they seem to endure.

CHAPTER 1

THE TWENTY-FOURTH STREET CORRIDOR

The corner of Twenty-Fourth Street at Castro Street has long been the busiest intersection in the heart of Noe Valley. This photograph, looking in a northeasterly direction, captures the aftermath of a June 1952 car crash in which the car in the background ran a stop sign, clipping the car in the foreground and causing it to flip over. Nobody was badly hurt. One of Noe Valley's two traffic lights has long since replaced the stop signs. (WNP.)

Looking east from Hoffman Street along the Twenty-Fourth Street corridor, we can almost make out the busy retail area, about five blocks down. Back in 1938, this was the end of the line for the Market Street Railway's No. 11 streetcar as it climbed westward from the Mission, and this corner store was a thriving concern. Today, this is the midpoint for the No. 48 bus line and the store has been repurposed. (WNP/WPY.)

In these views looking eastward from the southern shoulders of Twin Peaks, the unmistakable swaths of three major Noe Valley streets immediately below can be seen. Twenty-Third Street is on the left, and Twenty-Fourth Street is on the right. Between them, and appearing shorter than the others because it narrows at Sanchez Street, is Elizabeth Street. Most landmarks from 1953 are still visible today. St. Philip's Church is about halfway down Elizabeth. James Lick School is prominent about two blocks south of Twenty-Fourth Street. (WNP/WPY.)

THE TWENTY-FOURTH STREET CORRIDOR

These Victorian homes on Twenty-Fourth Street at the corner of Homestead Street are largely unchanged from 1944. At the top of the block is the corner grocery store at Twenty-Fourth and Hoffman Streets, which is seen from up the hill on page 12. The No. 11 streetcar seen here was the "Sunday Special," which went only as far as Mission Street. (WNP/WPY.)

The Noe Valley School, seen here on the northwest corner of Douglass Street and Twenty-Fourth, was a primary school that existed only from 1900 to 1926. It was demolished, and this site has long been occupied by Noe Courts, which includes tennis and basketball courts as well as this playground. The park is a favorite of all ages, especially toddlers and preschoolers. (Author's collection/WPY.)

THE TWENTY-FOURTH STREET CORRIDOR

As seen below in 1967, the Standard station at the corner of Twenty-fourth and Diamond Streets was replaced by an apartment house a few years later. The Victorian building across the street still stands, housing two popular eateries, and the spire of St. Philip's Church is prominent one block up the hill at Elizabeth Street in both pictures. (Author's collection/WPY.)

The above image, often identified as Twenty-Fourth Street at Diamond Street, is now thought to have been taken one block west at Twenty-Fourth and Douglass. This would have been before the buildings on the right were torn down to make way for The Noe Valley School in 1900. At this time Twenty-Fourth was still paved with stone. The streetcar rails are clearly visible, and Twin Peaks can be seen in the distance. (Author's collection/WPY.)

The Twenty-Fourth Street Corridor

Seen above in about 1965 at the same Standard station pictured on page 16 is the Pioneer, the first automobile to be produced on the West Coast. It was built by J.A. Meyer in 1896 in a garage on Twenty-Fourth Street, just a few doors away. Across the street, both the convent building of St. Philip's Parish and the Victorian building next door still stand. (Meyer family collection/WPY.)

The 1940s view below, looking westward up Twenty-Fourth Street toward Twin Peaks from Castro Street, shows a rail wrecker pulling an apparently disabled cable car on the tracks used by the Market Street Railway No. 11 streetcar. The contemporary view shows a Municipal Railway No. 48 bus. The buildings are largely unchanged. (WNP/WPY.)

The Twenty-Fourth Street Corridor   19

This three-story building at the southeast corner of Twenty-Fourth Street and Castro housed the Seymour Drug Company, a well-known Noe Valley business, from the turn of the 20th century into the 1970s. The corner has always been an important transit crossroads. In the 1927 photograph here are two westbound No. 11 streetcars on the left and a northbound Castro Street cable car on the right. The contemporary image shows a New Flyer XDE40 bus of the No. 48 Quintara line. (WNP/WPY.)

These views, looking across Castro Street, down Twenty-Fourth Street, were taken from roughly the same vantage point as those on the facing page. The photo above is cropped tighter than the one below. The corner buildings are still the same, and the Bank of America still does business in the one on the left. Cotton Basics now occupies the former Seymour Drug location. (Author's collection/WPY.)

THE TWENTY-FOURTH STREET CORRIDOR

In 1943, when the older photograph was taken, the recently built 4068 Twenty-Fourth Street (left) housed the Noe Valley Branch Post Office. On the right, 4066 Twenty-Fourth was built in 1904, survived the great earthquakes of 1906 and 1989, and was home to Pepe's Pool Hall from 1920 to 1954. The post office moved across the street in 1988, and a succession of retail shops followed. After Pepe, Ed Hogan Plumbing operated on the right from 1957 to 1979, and Small Frys children's store opened in 1984. (Author's collection/WPY.)

The businesses along the busy commercial corridor of the 4000 Block of Twenty-Fourth Street are always changing. The 1974 photograph here shows Surf Super, one of Noe Valley's fondly remembered small supermarkets. Inside was Reno's Meat Market, another favorite from an earlier era. This site now houses Wells Fargo Bank and Old Republic Title. (WPY/WPY.)

The heart of Noe Valley's shopping district is probably the corner of Twenty-Fourth and Noe Streets. In the photograph below from about 1944, a No. 11 Hoffman streetcar glides past the grand Noe Theater, the neighborhood's great movie palace, which was closed in 1952 and demolished. Charles Schroyer's Associated Service Station on the corner later became Flying A, then Rich's Philips 66. By 1974, when the photograph above was taken, it was Larry's Phillips 66. (Both, NVA.)

At the corner of Twenty-Fourth and Noe Streets, Larry's Phillips 66 closed in 1976, and Olympic Savings opened in this large new building in 1979. Since then, the bank has gone through a series of operators from Coast Savings to Home Savings to Washington Mutual, as seen here. After the latter collapsed in the largest bank failure in American history in 2008, its assets were taken over by Chase. (Both, WPY.)

THE TWENTY-FOURTH STREET CORRIDOR

In these "main street" views looking westward on Twenty-Fourth Street from Noe Street toward Twin Peaks, many of the buildings from the past are easily recognizable today. Back in 1926, the Palmer Theater, showing *For Heaven's Sake* starring Harold Lloyd, is on the left, and the Palmer Market is on the right. The former later became the Surf Super grocery, and it is now divided into a bank and title company. After a time as a bank, the Palmer Market site became locally owned Zephyr Real Estate. (NVA/WPY.)

Marching down Twenty-Fourth Street from Sanchez in April 1941, the St. Philip's School crossing guards carry shields that read "Forward Noe Valley." Many of the buildings from that era are recognizable today. On the corner, just to the left of the American flag, is the building that is now home to La Boulangerie coffee shop. In the distance, Twin Peaks was open space in 1941 but became heavily developed a few decades later. (NVA/WPY.)

THE TWENTY-FOURTH STREET CORRIDOR

Originally the Cook Shack, this diner at 3991 Twenty-Fourth Street was purchased by Herb and Margaret Gaines in 1945. For many of the years until Herb's Fine Foods closed in 2007, its lunch counter was the de facto center of Noe Valley civic life. In those days, it seemed that all the people most involved in neighborhood affairs met here routinely for morning coffee to hash out neighborhood affairs over plates of hash and hash browns. The site now houses the Toast Eatery, where Cash and his mother had just enjoyed breakfast when the author passed by to take this photo of his grandson and daughter. (Both, WPY.)

There was no place to park on Twenty-Fourth Street in "downtown Noe Valley" back in 1948, the year that Old Los Angeles with Paulette Goddard was playing at the Noe Theater. The No. 11 streetcar line was replaced by the No. 48 Quintara bus line, the theater was torn down, and some of the parking spaces were usurped by a "parklet" in front of the popular Just For Fun gift store. Old-timers still miss the gaudy and glamorous Noe. (WNP/WPY.)

THE TWENTY-FOURTH STREET CORRIDOR

Situated on Twenty-Fourth Street near Vicksburg, the Noe Valley Town Square is an active neighborhood gathering place, featuring a wide variety of community events from music, to children's programs, to movie night, and especially the weekly Noe Valley Farmer's Market. The tradition goes back to the 1940s, when Johnny McCarthy used to host an annual Christmas Puppet Show at his Shell gas station on this location. Today's murals are by artist Mona Caron. (NVA/WPY.)

As seen below, in the aftermath of the Loma Prieta Earthquake of October 17, 1989, the residents of Noe Valley lined up for coffee. Again as in 1906, Noe Valley suffered minimal earthquake damage. Spinelli's, which opened here on Twenty-Fourth Street near Sanchez in 1986, was superseded by Tully's in 1998 and became locally owned Bernie's (above) in 2007. Having started next door in 1968, Bell Market was replaced by Whole Foods in 2009. (Azia Yenne/WPY.)

The Twenty-Fourth Street Corridor

The retail space at the base of the Victorian building on the southeast corner of Twenty-Fourth Street and Noe has gone through a variety of incarnations. In 1974, when the photograph below was taken, Elisa Ining had her boutique here, and before that, it was Worthington's. In 1978, it was home to Gifts of the Magi, the first iteration of the captivating Star Magic gift store, which later had a two-decade run a half block to the west. Starbucks moved into the location in 1993. (NVA/WPY.)

In the top photo, an unidentified uniformed group, looking like a marching band without instruments, advances westward on Twenty-Fourth Street through its intersection with Sanchez Street. The buildings on the corner remain immediately recognizable today. (WNP/WPY.)

The Twenty-Fourth Street Corridor

The imposing Victorian building that dominated the corner of Twenty-Fourth Street at Church Street in 1907 remains. Back then, J. Lang's tavern—selling National Lager and Steam Beer—was on the ground floor corner, and Oakwood Market occupied the Twenty-Fourth Street side. Happy Donuts has occupied the corner spot since the late 20th century, and Shufat Market has operated on the Twenty-Fourth side since 1972. Dr. Schultz, the dentist, has no current successor, as second-floor businesses are officially discouraged in Noe Valley. (NVA/WPY.)

CHAPTER 2

NORTH OF TWENTY-FOURTH

This is the view looking south from Alvarado Street toward St. Philip's Church on the morning after the famous February 1976 San Francisco snowstorm. In this image, the snow, which had amounted to a few inches, had melted from Diamond Street, but it remained on the rooftops. In shady areas, such as in backyards, it took three days to disappear. Snow flurries still occur every few years, but since 1976 there has been no appreciable accumulation. (WPY.)

In the westward vista from the top of the Twenty-Second Street Steps, near where Twenty-Second intersects Collingwood Street, one can contemplate what has changed since 1935. The massive Alvarado School, built in 1926 south of Twenty-Second, is still prominent. The Victorian homes in the valley and the lower hillsides remain, but substantial development took place on Twin Peaks in the 1960s. (WNP/WPY.)

In these photographs, one from the 1930s and one from today, we look northeasterly from Portola Drive toward the downtown skyline on the left. The hill from which the photographs on the facing page were taken is in the center, with Alvarado School slightly below and to the left. St. Philip's Church on Diamond Street can be seen at the far right edge of both pictures. (WNP/WPY.)

On northbound Twenty-First Street, as it nears the transition from Noe Valley to Eureka Valley, the Douglass Street right-of-way was forked in 1926 because of the slope of the hillside. At the top of the block, the left-hand fork makes a hard left into Romain Street. The photograph above shows the completed, paved street in 1927. (DPW/WPY.)

A pair of Victorian homes on the steep part of Twenty-Second Street west of Castro Street. Back in 1920, before grading, this was not so much a street of a trail with a steep, rickety, wooden staircase leading up to Collingwood Street. Today, it is paved but no less steep. There is still a staircase, but it is concrete with a metal railing. (DPW/WPY.)

These are good views looking south, down into Noe Valley along the route of the Market Street Railway's Castro Street cable car line. The cable car was phased out in 1941, and the route has long been served by the San Francisco Municipal Railway's No. 24 Divisadero bus line. Many of the Victorian buildings in the foreground remain unchanged since 1940—or indeed since the 1890s—but on the background hillsides, there has been much development in the ensuing years. (NVA/WPY.)

Until 1941, the Market Street Railway's Castro Street cable car made its southbound run across the top of the hill between Market Street and Noe Valley. Today, the San Francisco Municipal Railway's No. 24 Divisadero bus makes this run. These photographs were taken about a block north of those on the facing page and looking in the opposite direction. The homes, dating from the 1920s, remain generally unchanged except for their garage doors. (WNP/WPY.)

North of Twenty-Fourth

Originally built in 1909, this San Francisco Fire Department station opened in 1910 with Engine No. 11 and transitioned to Engine No. 44 in 1916. The building was sold to artists Mark Adams and Beth Van Hoesen in 1959. Having changed hands several times, it has been remodeled into a luxury home. (NVA/WPY.)

In the photograph above, Ace and Axel, two neighborhood kids, and their mom stroll past the fire station at Alvarado Street and Hoffman that houses the San Francisco Fire Department Engine 24 and two reserve pumpers. The engine pictured here joined the department in 2006, the centennial of the Great Earthquake and Fire. The station was originally constructed in 1914, the date of the photograph below, and enlarged in 1997. (NVA/WPY.)

This substantial building on the northwest corner of Twenty-Third and Douglass Streets was built in 1912 and housed the Wieger & Hagermann Grocery through 1933. The business has gone through a number of name changes through the years, being known as Norman's Groceteria between 1957 and 1973 and as Sunshine Market for many years after 1982. (NVA/WPY.)

Originally founded around 1892 across Chattanooga Street, the F. Hartje Grocery Store moved to this location on the northwest corner of Chattanooga and Twenty-Second Streets around 1903. Fred Hartje, probably the man to the left of the light pole, later served as treasurer of the Retail Grocers Association of San Francisco. This drastically modified former retail space is now a residence. (NVA/WPY.)

North of Twenty-Fourth

Once, the culture embraced celebratory parades for almost anything. The one in the photograph above, coming down Diamond Street from Elizabeth Street in May 1938 with a substantial marching band, was being held to celebrate the opening of the "Eureka-Diamond" bus line, roughly analogous to the route now served by the San Francisco Municipal Railway's No. 35 Eureka line. St. Philip's Church is prominent in the center of both pictures. Most of the buildings (including the author's home on the hill in the background) still remain, but there are many more trees. (WNP/WPY.)

CHAPTER 3

THE CHURCH STREET CORRIDOR

The 1950 "Bullet Nose" Studebaker at the curb helps to date this undated photograph of a streetcar of the San Francisco Municipal Railway's J Church line as it makes its way southbound along Church Street from Twenty-Second Street toward Twenty-Third Street. The J Church line began service from downtown to Thirtieth Street in 1916. The tracks were extended south to the Balboa Park Bay Area Rapid Transit (BART) Station in 1991, but routine J Church service on the new tracks did not commence until June 1993. (WNP.)

The J Church streetcar is seen here approaching Thirtieth Street at the southern end of Church Street. In February 1960, it was a classic PCC car. Today, it is one of the Siemens S200 cars that began service in 2017. The buildings remain largely unchanged, though their usage has evolved. Johnnie's Fountain Grill went through numerous changes before becoming the upscale Pomelo. (WNP/WPY.)

In these images, we can compare transit vehicles on Thirtieth Street crossing the end of the Church Street corridor more than a half century apart. Above is a J Church PCC streetcar in the 1960s, while below there is a modern New Flyer XT40 of the San Francisco Municipal Railway's No. 24 Divisadero bus line. (WNP/WPY.)

The Church Street Corridor

The J Church streetcar glides past Twenty-Eighth Street as it dashes north on Church Street with the spires of St. Paul's Catholic Church prominent in the background. The three-story Victorian apartment house on the corner remains, but the building across the street is gone. Originally it was the Rita Theater, specializing in German language films, but by the early 1960s, it had become the Holiness Temple in Christ. In the 1990s, when the author had his offices across the intersection, it had been painted bright blue and repurposed as the Church At San Francisco. Two decades later, it was replaced by an apartment house built in the slick modern style now demanded by the San Francisco Planning Department. (WNP/WPY.)

St. Paul's Catholic Church, a 1,400-seat English Gothic structure at the corner of Valley Street and Church was dedicated in 1911 after 14 years under construction. Its tallest spire, which is 365 feet high, makes it the tallest structure in Noe Valley, though it is in the valley, and most of the surrounding hills are higher. The church was featured in the popular 1992 musical comedy film *Sister Act*. (NVA/WPY.)

As seen here in 1951, Gene Paridy's Chevron Service Station was located on the southeast corner of Day and Church Streets. A decade later, it was torn down and replaced by this four-unit apartment building. It was one of five gas stations in Noe Valley. (Assessor's Office/WPY.)

These images show J Church streetcars heading south just past Twenty-Sixth Street. In 1949, there were fewer trees and more parking. Though the building on the corner is partially obscured by one of those trees, there is no doubt that it is the same one. (WNP/WPY.)

THE CHURCH STREET CORRIDOR

These views look north along Church Street from near the narrow alley known as Comerford Street. In the February 1916 photograph, the street was being excavated, possibly for the laying of rails for the streetcar line. As with many photographs on these pages, the addition of street trees to the area is underscored dramatically by comparing these photographs. (DPW/WPY.)

Two streetcars, a classic PCC car and a modern Breda LRV, make the stop at the busy corner of Church Street and Twenty-Fourth, one of the crossroads of Noe Valley. The 1965 Dodge Monaco helps to date the image below. The spires of St. Paul's Church, seen in the distance in both pictures, are an easy reference point for comparison. The PCC cars were named for the Presidents' Conference Committee, a group of urban transit agency presidents who developed a standardized design for a quiet, streamlined streetcar. Used in more than 30 cities, PCC cars entered service in San Francisco in 1939 and served routinely with Muni into the 1970s. Some are still in service as part of Muni's "historic streetcar" fleet. (WNP/WPY.)

THE CHURCH STREET CORRIDOR

These views looking south on Church Street at the corner of Twenty-Second Street show the J Church streetcar right-of-way emerging onto Church on the run from Dolores Park, after passing through backyards in order to avoid the hill. In June 1916, the rails were still being laid. (United Railroads/WPY.)

CHAPTER 4

SOUTHWARD INTO UPPER NOE

Douglass Playground at Douglass Street and Twenty-Sixth was part of a series of federal Works Progress Administration projects undertaken in San Francisco between 1935 and 1939. Here, 5,700 cubic yards of loose rock were removed from an old quarry, 3,500 feet of irrigation pipe were placed, and the still extant clubhouse seen here was built. (WNP/WPY.)

Completed in 1888, the Market Street Railway's Castro Street cable car barn was located a block south of Twenty-Fourth Street at Jersey Street. After the cable cars stopped running in 1941, it became a Safeway, then the Little Bell Market, and finally Walgreens. Most of the other buildings present in the 1940s are still here. (WNP/WPY.)

Seen here is a Market Street Railway work car (note the MSRY logo on the door) at Castro and Jersey Streets. The 1880s Victorian building on the northwest corner is still there, but its cupola is gone. Back in 1941, there were no homes on Twin Peaks (left background), but this rapidly changed after World War II. (WNP/WPY.)

On this page, a photograph of street work in progress around the cable car turntable at Twenty-Sixth and Castro Streets in January 1916 is compared to one of the same scenes today. The buildings remain the same, though the modes of transit have evolved. The Castro Street cable car last turned on this table in 1941. (United Railroads/WPY.)

Looking north on Castro Street from Twenty-Sixth, we see the cable car turntable as it existed in 1940, and the same well-worn location as it is today. The building on the right that once housed H.C. Schmidt Liquor, and which now is home to Angel's Market, has changed somewhat over the years. However, compare these photos to the one of the same location at the top of page 62. (WNP/WPY.)

Southward into Upper Noe

Here, the Castro Street cable car on its turntable at Twenty-Sixth Street in 1938 is compared to a modern New Flyer XT40 of the San Francisco Municipal Railway's No. 24 Divisadero bus line in exactly the same spot. The building on the corner was about to undergo extensive remodeling to give it a "Forties Modern" facade. (WNP/WPY.)

The last cable car to serve Noe Valley is seen in the image below as it begins its final northbound run from Twenty-Sixth Street on the afternoon of April 5, 1941. The same Victorian apartment house on the corner remains today, but it is now obscured by trees. (WNP/WPY.)

SOUTHWARD INTO UPPER NOE

These pictures from the southern shoulder of Twin Peaks look southeasterly across Noe Valley toward San Francisco Bay. Bernal Heights is at the top center, and the dark slope leading down toward Douglass Park is on the right. Twenty-Second Street is at the left edge of the August 1946 picture, and Elizabeth Street is on the left of the contemporary view. Below, Portola Drive, once easily seen from here, is now largely obscured. (WNP/WPY.)

Here, we look north from Diamond Heights across the western edge of Noe Valley toward where Market Street becomes Portola Drive, with Twin Peaks to the left above. For orientation, Fountain Street, ending at Twenty-Fourth Street, can be easily seen in the lower right corner of both the March 1921 photograph and the current view. (DPW/WPY.)

SOUTHWARD INTO UPPER NOE

The above image, taken from Diamond Heights in March 1940, shows a sliver of the recently completed Clipper Street Extension. This picture provides a feel for these hills in the days before the construction of this prominent thoroughfare, which is clearly visible in the modern photograph. (DPW/WPY.)

This is the familiar view looking down Clipper Street toward Noe Valley and the downtown skyline, as seen in 1940 and today. The Clipper Street Extension gave Noe Valley easy access to the western parts of the city. The intersection between Clipper and Portola Dive, which is to the left and behind us, was long ago realigned and the curve in Clipper straightened. (WNP/WPY.)

These images look north, down Douglass Street from near Twenty-Seventh Street, with Douglass Park to the west. The park was built as part of a federal Works Progress Administration project between 1935 and 1939. Since that time, huge stands of cypress trees have grown up on all sides of this popular park. (WNP/WPY.)

This is the view looking down into Noe Valley from Portola Drive, with Bernal Heights at the top center. James Lick School, between Twenty-Fifth and Clipper Streets, is easily seen at center left. The street at the center of the top photo is Clipper as it existed before work on the Clipper Street Extension was begun. The barren hillside on the right in the June 1937 image is now the cypress forest lying uphill from Douglass Park. (DPW/WPY.)

Southward into Upper Noe   69

This Mid-Century Modern home at the corner of Twenty-Sixth Street and Douglass, built in 1950, still stands, surrounded by many of the same houses that were there at mid-century. (Assessor's Office/WPY.)

This line of Victorian homes along Noe Street, from Valley Street uphill to Twenty-Eighth, is remarkably unchanged after more than a century since they were photographed in January 1917. The street, however, was paved long ago. The official city records show that by 1928, this block of Valley Street was paved with asphalt, but the next block downhill toward Twenty-Ninth was still paved with brick. (DPW/WPY.)

Southward into Upper Noe

The photograph below of a lady in her roadster climbing Duncan Street to Noe Street in about 1923 is one of our favorite images from the Noe Valley of yore. Noe Street was not yet paved, but Duncan, like many of the steepest streets, was paved with stones. By the 1950s, this block of Duncan was closed and replaced by pedestrian steps. (NVA/WPY.)

In 1937, the corner of Dolores Street and Twenty-Seventh still lay beneath a trestle built by the Southern Pacific Railroad. This line sliced through numerous housing blocks as it made its way southwesterly from the industrial districts south of Market Street as it headed into the Bernal Cut toward points south. The rails were gradually replaced by the construction of San Jose Avenue in the 1930s. Eventually, the tracks and trestles disappeared, and today there is little evidence of this ever having been a rail corridor. After more than eight decades, however, the houses remain virtually unchanged. With its palm-lined median, Dolores is a handsome thoroughfare. (WNP/WPY.)

Southward into Upper Noe

This Mid-Century Modern home was built on Douglass Street on the shoulder of Diamond Heights overlooking the southern end of Noe Valley. When it was photographed in 1951, it stood out prominently, but over time, larger buildings, a fence, and foliage gradually encircled it, blending it into the surrounding landscape. (Assessor's Office/WPY.)

This view is from the top of Duncan Street, looking down across Noe Street toward Upper Noe. Holly Park is in the distance in the center of the August 1936 image and on the right in the contemporary image. The spires of St. Paul's Church are visible in both. The house pictured on page 72 is in the lower left of the modern photograph. (WNP/WPY.)

SOUTHWARD INTO UPPER NOE

This is a view looking westward on Twenty-Seventh Street in October 1940 and today. The small home on the right remains. From this intersection, Castro Street runs downhill, and Newburg Street runs uphill. Newburg is in almost perfect alignment with the roadway of the San Francisco–Oakland Bay Bridge, five miles to the northeast. (DPW/WPY.)

No reference points other than the contour of the land remain from October 1940 as we look eastward along Twenty-Seventh Street in the opposite direction as the view on the facing page. Diamond Street is the first street below us in the modern photograph, with Castro Street a block beyond. Much development occurred here in the years immediately after World War II. (DPW/WPY.)

Southward into Upper Noe

In these photographs looking eastward along Twenty-Ninth Street from near the corner of Noe, Bernal Heights is prominent in the center. In 1938, the Market Street Railway's No. 9 streetcar traveled up and down to this intersection on a single track but was double tracked from Sanchez Street, one block down the hill. Today, the No. 24 Divisadero bus line crosses through here on Noe. Most of the buildings from that earlier era remain. (WNP/WPY.)

In a reverse of the pictures on the facing page, the view looks uphill on Twenty-Ninth Street from Sanchez, westward toward Gold Mike Hill. There was a lot of street work ongoing here in January 1939. Unlike other photograph pairs in this book, there are few landmarks in common between these two. (DPW/WPY.)

Southward into Upper Noe

Both views here look westward up the last block of Valley Street from Castro Street toward Gold Mine Hill. In 1923, this block remained an unpaved dirt road. On Halloween 1929, city photographer Horace Chaffee documented the block again after it had been recently paved. The buildings are familiar, but there was now a concrete stairway on the right. (DPW/DPW.)

As late as 1998, the author was able to document the last block of Valley Street and find some of the same buildings that were seen here back in 1923 and when Chaffee visited the intersection in 1929. However, today, virtually all the buildings have changed. (WPY/WPY.)

Southward into Upper Noe

From a vantage point on the rocky cliffs of Billy Goat Hill, we look north into Upper Noe. The prominent street on the left is the last block of Castro Street. In the 1915 image, the curving dirt road entering the frame from the lower right is Day Street, which is obscured by trees in the modern photo. Castro and Day intersect with one another at Twenty-Ninth Street, which crosses from left to right in the center of the picture. Many of the houses on Twenty-Ninth can be seen in both pictures. (WNP/WPY.)

SOUTHWARD INTO UPPER NOE

These pictures look south from the intersection of Castro and Day Streets, back up toward the vantage point of the facing page photos on Billy Goat Hill. By June 1930, the streets were paved and the concrete railing had been installed. The building at the corner on the right is in both of these photos, though it had not yet been built in 1915. (DPW/WPY.)

SOUTHWARD INTO UPPER NOE

Many of the buildings at the corner of Twenty-Ninth and Noe Streets, especially the distinctive apartment house on the right, still exist. However, the Market Street Railway No. 9 streetcar long ago ceased making its run from this corner, by way of Valencia Street, to the Ferry Building. (WNP/WPY.)

By some reckoning, Laidley Street is in Glen Park, but others say it is in Upper Noe. One must look carefully to identify the buildings that still survive from April 1926, but the divided routing of Laidley Street, as seen from our vantage point looking northwest from Noe Street is still essentially the same. In the 1920s, many of the streets in Upper Noe and the higher parts of Glen Park to the south remained as dirt roads. Billy Goat Hill is in the near distance, with Twin Peaks beyond. They are easily identified in the background of the 1926 image but now somewhat obscured by trees and buildings. Today, Sutro Tower, located two miles to the northwest, across Twin Peaks, is a prominent feature. (DPW/WPY.)

This view looks westward, up Thirtieth Street from Noe to the Laidley Street intersection. Billy Goat Hill rises above this intersection, with Gold Mine Hill above that. When the picture above was taken in August 1927, Gold Mine Hill was still pasture land. This changed dramatically in the 1960s. The yard of the Kate Kennedy School is on the right. (DPW/WPY.)

The point where Thirtieth Street curves sharply around the base of Billy Goat Hill can be seen at the top of Thirtieth in the picture on the facing page. Unpaved in August 1927, this winding block is now paved—and urbanized with many parked cars. Though a time traveler from that era would recognize Billy Goat Hill, few human-made structures remain here from 1927. (DPW/WPY.)

Southward into Upper Noe

The August 1927 photograph above shows how Day Street was constructed to snake between Thirtieth Street (foreground) and Twenty-Ninth and emerge at the intersection of Twenty-Ninth and Castro Streets. In the contemporary photograph, most of Day Street is obscured by trees. In 1927, these blocks of Castro and Thirtieth Streets still remained unpaved. (DPW/WPY.)

Here is a view of Thirtieth Street near Noe that is similar to that portrayed by the photographs on page 86, but this time looking southwesterly toward Gold Mine Hill. The building at the center provides a good reference point. Curiously, at some time between the 1930s and today, all of these homes paved their front yards. (Bruce Dettman Collection/WPY.)

SOUTHWARD INTO UPPER NOE

Looking eastward along Thirtieth Street toward Bernal Heights, we have a good view of San Francisco Municipal Railway electrified transit of eras more than half a century apart. In the photograph above, it is a PCC streetcar of the J Line, around 1960, while below is a New Flyer XT40 electrified bus of the No. 24 Divisadero bus line. Today, the Bernal Heights radio tower in the distance is surrounded by trees. (WNP/WPY.)

This is the view looking westward into Upper Noe from Bernal Heights, in 1950 and today, with many more trees. Thirtieth Street, prominent in the center, leads up toward Gold Mine Hill, with Mount Davidson behind and slightly to the left. Kate Kennedy School, on the right side of Thirtieth (bright yellow in the contemporary picture), is prominent, as is St. Paul's Church on the right side of both frames. (Author's collection/WPY.)

Southward into Upper Noe

The area at the head of Thirtieth Street, after it twists around the base of Billy Goat Hill, was once home to the Gray Brothers Quarry. In 1914, shortly before the top photograph was taken, millionaire owner George Gray was murdered here by Joseph LoCoco in a wage dispute. The quarry, which remained until the 1940s, was long ago replaced by new housing up the side of Gold Mine Hill, but the home in the center with the pyramidal roof remains as a reference feature. (NVA/WPY.)

CHAPTER 5

SELECTED NOE VALLEY MAPS

Dating from 1863, this map of Horner's Addition shows the street names that John Meirs Horner originally assigned. As indicated in red by the author, new names and numbers were later assigned, appearing as early as 1870. Horner's Park Street became Twenty-Fourth Street, but Elizabeth Street, named for his wife, remains. Horner's Diamond Street became Castro Street, but a new street, one block to the west became a new Diamond Street. North is to the right on this map. (Author's collection, with author additions.)

One of several "homestead" developments within present Noe Valley was the Noe Garden district laid out by eccentric financier F.L.A. Pioche. Surveyed in March–April 1869, the plan was filed with the county recorder in August 1869. Indicated in red are present names. North is at the top on this map. (Author's collection, with author additions.)